Contents

Say the Sounds   4

Tricky Words   5

Spot the Story Setting   6

The Enormous Turnip   7

Rumpelstiltskin   25

Puppets   43

Many More Monsters   61

The Pumpkin Party   79

Town Mouse and Country
Mouse   97

Book Review   116

Character Review   118

This book belongs to

D1322528

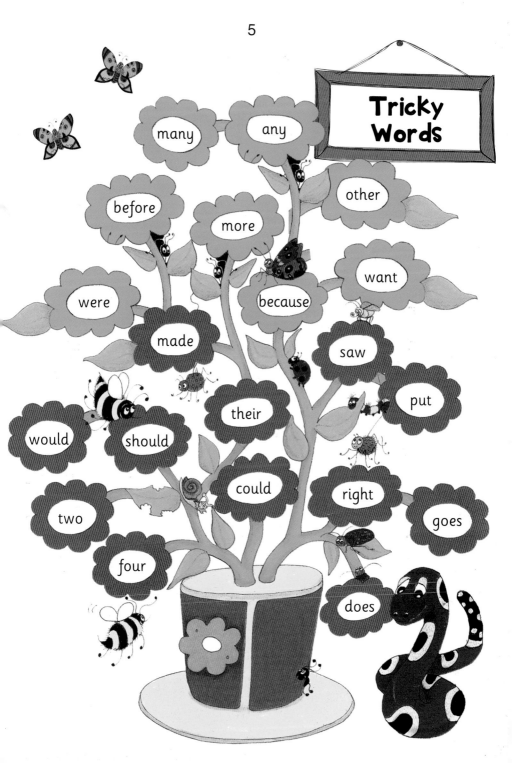

Tricky Words

many

any

other

before

more

want

were

because

made

saw

put

would

should

their

could

right

goes

two

four

does

Spot the Story Setting

shed

garden

classroom

town house

cave

mill

The Enormous Turnip

er

pepper   smaller
butter   bigger
her   winter
dinner   burgers
shudder   fritters
corner   casserole
perch

girl
shirt
dirty
stirred

ir

ur

turnips
nurse
purple
turkey
burgers

An old man lived in a small house with a big garden. He was very proud of his garden. There were rows of carrots, big round pumpkins, plump corn cobs, peas and turnips.

As he looked at the things growing
in his garden, the old man saw that
one of the turnips seemed to be
bigger than the others.
Every time he looked at the turnip,
it had grown bigger.

The turnip got
bigger
and
bigger
and
bigger
until it was
enormous.

The enormous turnip sat in the middle of the old man's garden. Its leaves were as big as trees.
The turnip was *so* enormous that everyone would stop and gaze at it.

One morning, the old man looked
out of his window.
"It's time that turnip came up," he
said to himself.

So he put on his boots and strode
outside. He took hold of the turnip and
tugged and tugged. He went around to
the other side and tugged and tugged,
but the turnip was stuck in the ground.

The old man scratched his head and
then he went and got his spade. He
dug all around the enormous turnip.
It took him a long time.
When he had finished, he took hold
of the turnip and tried again, but the
turnip was still stuck.

A nurse, who was on her way home, looked into the garden and saw the enormous turnip and the old man. She went to help. She held on to the old man's waist and the two of them tugged and tugged, but the turnip was still stuck in the ground.

A little girl skipped along the lane.
She saw the old man and the nurse
and went to help too.
The old man, the nurse and the
little girl tugged and tugged,
but the turnip was still stuck.

A little boy in a green shirt ran along
the lane. He stopped when he saw the
enormous turnip, the old man
and the others.
"Do you want any help?"
he shouted to them.

So the little boy went to help the old
man, the nurse and the little girl.
The four of them tugged and tugged,
but the turnip was still stuck.

A big dog with a wide purple collar
ran down the lane. He, too, stopped
when he saw everyone in the garden.
"I am big and strong," he barked.
"I will come and help."
So the old man, the nurse, the little
girl, the little boy and the dog tugged
and tugged. But it was no good;
the turnip was still stuck.

The old man had a big turkey, who
lived in a shed in the garden. The
turkey had seen what was happening.
"Gobble, gobble," he said,
and joined the line.
So the turkey, the dog, the little boy,
the little girl, the nurse and the old man
all tugged, but it was still no good.

A hen had been looking down from her perch on the wall.
"If that turkey can help, then so can I," she clucked.
She flapped down and went to help.
She held on to turkey, who held on to dog, who held on to the little boy, who held on to the little girl, who held on to the nurse, who held on to the old man.

But the turnip was still stuck!

A dirty black and white cat was out mousing. He rushed around the corner and stopped when he saw the enormous turnip.

"Come and help," called the nurse.

So the dirty cat joined the hen, the turkey, the dog, the little boy, the little girl, the nurse and the old man. They all tugged and tugged and grunted and groaned.

Suddenly, the turnip gave a little
shudder. Then it started to wobble.
Then, PLOP! The enormous turnip
popped out of the ground.

The cat,
the hen,
the turkey,
the dog,
the little boy,
the little girl,
the nurse and the old man
all shouted and tumbled to the ground.

"Thank you," said the old man.
"You must all come to dinner."
So the old man peeled the enormous
turnip and chopped it up into smaller
bits. Then he boiled and mashed and
stirred and fried. He added garlic and
butter and pepper and mustard.
When it was ready, the friends all sat
down to dinner. There was plenty for all.

In fact, there was so much of it that
the old man ate turnip all winter long.
He had turnip salad, turnip pie, turnip
sandwiches, turnip pancakes, turnip
burgers, turnip fritters, turnip curry,
mashed turnip and turnip casserole!

What's in the book?

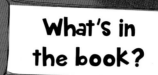

What does the old man grow in his garden?

Who is the first person to try and help the old man?

Why does the dog think he can help?

What do you think?

Why does the old man dig all around the turnip?

Why does the old man invite all the helpers to dinner?

Rumpelstiltskin

all
talk
small
walked

daughter
fault

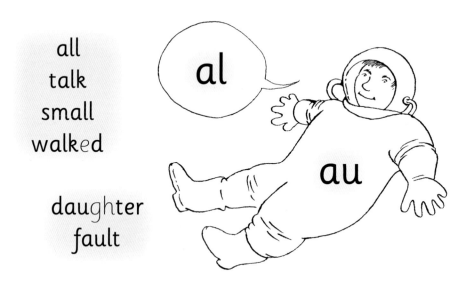

saw
dawn
straw
yawned

A long time ago, there lived a miller.
As he ground the wheat into flour at
his mill, he would talk to whoever was
with him. He would start telling them
about something that had happened,
but then he would add things to the
story, boasting as he went.

One day, a man came to the miller with some wheat. The miller started telling the man all about his daughter. He told him how witty and clever she was. The miller got more and more carried away until he found himself telling the man that his daughter was so clever she could spin straw into gold.

The next day, the man walked back into the mill. He was a servant of the King, and he had told him all about the miller and his daughter. The King had been so impressed he had sent his servant back with orders that the miller's daughter should come and see him.

"I would like you to spin all of this straw into gold for me," ordered the King, pointing to a pile of straw. He smiled and said, "I will see you and the gold in the morning."

Then he added, "If you do not do this, I shall have the miller thrown into jail for telling me lies!" and with that he shut the door.

The girl groaned. Why did the miller
have to say these silly things?
She was stuck here and it was all the
miller's fault. She could not spin straw
into gold. She sat alone by the
spinning wheel and cried.

"Excuse me," said someone, "can I help?" The girl looked up. She saw a short man standing on the pile of straw, looking down at her.

"No one can help me," she cried. "The King wants me to spin this straw into gold by morning."

The short man nodded and smiled.
"If I spin this straw into gold for you,
what will you pay me?" he said to
her. She looked up at him.
"I have this pendant," she replied,
and held it out to him.

When she awoke at dawn the next morning, the girl yawned and looked about. The little man had gone and so had the straw. Instead, there were spools of gold, glistening in the morning sun. The King was very impressed.

The next day, the King showed the
miller's daughter to the room again.
In one small corner was the spinning
wheel, but the rest of the room
was piled with straw.
"Spin this into gold for me," said the
King, "and I will let you go home."

Again, the girl sat at the spinning wheel and cried. Again, when she looked up, there was the short man, standing on the straw.

"I do not have anything to give you this time," she sobbed.
"I will still spin this for you, if you promise to give me your first born babe," said the man.

The next day, the King was so
pleased with the gold that he
married the Miller's daughter,
and they were very happy.

The Queen forgot all about the
funny, short man who had helped her
until, one morning, she found
him in her room.
"I have come to collect your first
born babe," he said.

The Queen cried and pleaded with him.
The little man took pity on her.
"If you can guess my name, you can
keep the babe," he said.
The Queen tried to guess, but each time
she said a name he shook his head.

Then he vanished.

The next day, the King and Queen
sent out some of the servants to
collect names. But that evening, as
the Queen read each name on her list,
the little man shook his head.

"Sorry," he said, "you have still not
guessed my name.
I will give you one more day."

The next day, all of the servants were
sent out to collect more names.
One of them was on his way back
when he stopped and listened.
Someone was singing.

"I spun, I spun the straw into gold.
The Queen, the Queen must never be
told my name is Rumpelstiltskin."

That evening, the Queen began
the list of names.

"NO, NO, NO!" shouted the little man.
"Then is your name *Rumpelstiltskin*?"
she said. The little man stopped.
Then he started to stomp and stamp,
and get very angry. He shouted and
stormed until, with a mighty stomp and
a yell, he was gone, and the Queen
never saw him again.

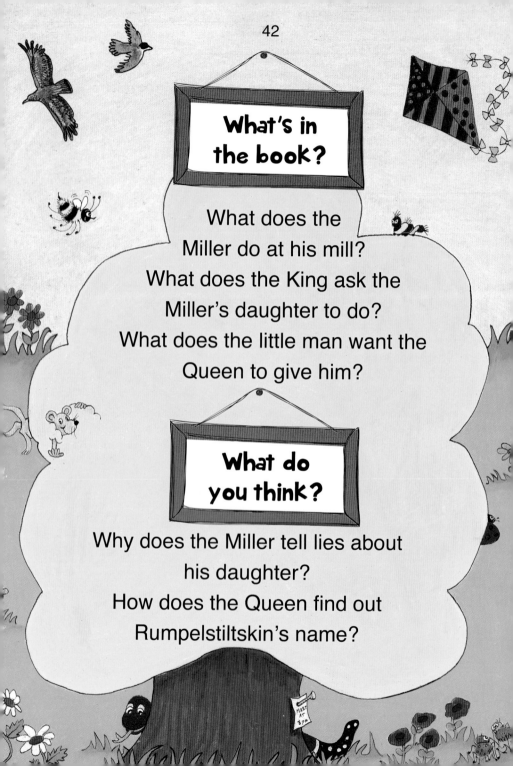

What's in the book?

What does the Miller do at his mill?
What does the King ask the Miller's daughter to do?
What does the little man want the Queen to give him?

What do you think?

Why does the Miller tell lies about his daughter?
How does the Queen find out Rumpelstiltskin's name?

Puppets

The windows by Miss Beech's desk looked out across the school grounds to the gates. Everyone who visited the school had to go by.

Every Thursday, the school delivery
van would arrive. Every Thursday, the
children in Miss Beech's class would
look out for the van. When it arrived,
they would giggle and wave.

Miss Beech could not understand why the children liked the delivery van's visit so much. When she looked out of the window, all she could see was the delivery van and a man unloading boxes from the back.

On Thursday mornings, the children wrote stories and Miss Beech would listen to them read.
As the hands of the clock made their way up to ten o'clock, the children would start looking out of the windows, waiting for the van to arrive.

"There he is!" the children would whisper, and look up.

This Thursday morning was
exactly the same.
"He's got a flag today,"
whispered Gus to Anna,
and all the children waved.

Miss Beech told Seth to stop reading
and turned to look out of the window.
All she could see was the man
unloading the van.
"Flag? Who has a flag?"
frowned Miss Beech.

Miss Beech was determined to solve the
puzzle. What was it about the delivery
van that the children liked so much?
"Next Thursday, I will see,"
she promised herself.

So, the following Thursday, Miss
Beech settled the children down to
write their stories about a man with a
van. Then she listened to some of the
children reading their books.
As ten o'clock approached,
Miss Beech sent Bill back to his seat.

This week, when the delivery man arrived, Miss Beech was looking out of the window too. As the van turned into the school, a puppet dog looked out of the van window and waved a wooden spoon.

The children all started giggling and pointing. When Miss Beech stood up, the puppet vanished.

The man got out of the van and started unloading the boxes. Miss Beech sat down again. When the van left, the puppet waved to the children again.

"So that's it!" exclaimed Miss Beech.
"Does the puppet wave every week?"
she said.
"Yes," replied Seth, "and every week he
has something different in his paws."

"Yes, he has had a hat with a red ribbon on it..." said Hinda.
"...and he had a big paintbrush one week," added Rob.

"I liked the yellow sunflower," said Kim.
"No, the bucket and spade were best!" said Meg.

"Well, goodness me!" cried Miss Beech.
"I have been missing out."

"Yes, every week we try to guess what
the dog will have," said Meg.
"I think we will make our own surprise
for the man in the van,"
smiled Miss Beech.

First, they talked about what they were going to do. Then the children and Miss Beech started to make plans.
By the end of the lesson, all the children had a pattern of what they were going to make.

In the next lesson, they each started to make something. Miss Beech lifted down the big bag of felt and scraps, and the children started cutting and sticking and stitching.

"They are going to be very good," said Miss Beech, as she went around the room. "I cannot wait to see them finished." All the children agreed.

When Thursday morning came,
the children could hardly contain
themselves. The hands on the clock
seemed very slow that morning.

Then the van turned into the car park.
Out of the van window, the puppet dog
started to wave. All the children rushed
to the windows and waved back with
the puppets they had made!

The man in the van grinned and took his puppet dog out from the cab of the van. He came across to the window and he looked at the puppets that the children had made.
"As well as being very surprised, I am very, *very* impressed!" he said.

What's in the book?

What do the children do in class on Thursday mornings?
What things has the delivery man's puppets had?
What sort of puppets do the children make?

What do you think?

Why do the children look forward to Thursday mornings?
Why has Miss Beech not seen the puppet before?

Many More Monsters

I saw a monster

I saw a monster with two tails,
four arms and crimson scales.
Another monster, off to play,
jumped and giggled all the way.

I saw a monster, big and green,
munching on a butter bean.

Another monster, with sharp teeth,
was eating up a massive feast.

I saw a monster, in a tie,
looking up into the sky.

Another monster was flying a kite.
Look out monster! Hold on tight!

I saw a monster,
in a coat,
slowly reading
a little note.

Another monster,
in the snow,
was shivering
from head to toe.

I saw a monster, sad and blue,
playing softly on a flute.
Another monster, just on cue,
was bringing in a steaming stew.

I saw a monster, name of Roy,
sit and destroy a monster toy.
Another monster, black as oil,
waited for the kettle to boil.

I saw a monster, big and stout,
row and scream and loudly shout.
Another monster, with a scowl,
opened his mouth and began to howl.

I saw a monster
with a curl.
I think she must
have been a girl.

Another monster,
her little sister,
turned and twirled
and got a blister.

I saw a monster, with a horn,
snort, then pause, then talk till dawn.

Another monster, big and tall,
fell asleep against a wall.

Any Many and the other, his brother, Many More

Any Many Monster
liked to yell and snarl.
"I would snarl, I could snarl,
I should snarl," he yelled.

Any Many Monster
never saw any others.
Where does a monster like that
go to meet another?

Any Many Monster
liked to be alone.
"I could be alone, I should be alone,
I would be alone," he snarled.

But Any Many Monster
really wanted a friend.
Where does a monster like that
go to meet some others?

Then, one morning, Any Many
was jolted wide awake.
"I would snap, I could shout,
I should moan," he yelled.

When Any Many Monster
looked out from his cave,
another monster stood there.
Each looked at the other.

Any Many Monster
started to snarl and yell,
but then... "I could, I would,
I should recognise that monster!

It is no other than my brother.
My little brother, Many More.
It is you and no other, isn't it?
It is you, Many More!"

Any Many Monster
hugged his brother, Many More.
"I should cry, I would cry,
I could cry," he snuffled.

Then Any Many and Many More
looked at one another.
They hugged and hissed, and
cried and snarled, and yelled...

...and yelled, and snarled and cried, and hissed and hugged.

They lived, one bad-tempered
monster with another,
and argued and shouted,
and ranted and raved
quite happily with each other!

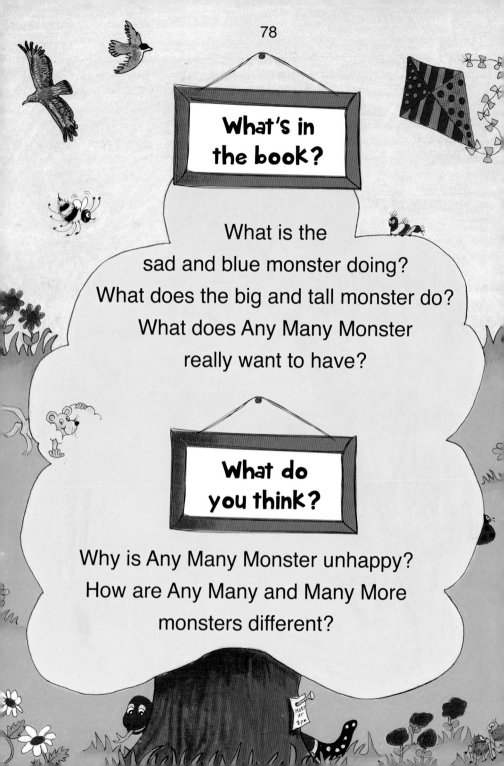

What's in the book?

What is the
sad and blue monster doing?
What does the big and tall monster do?
What does Any Many Monster
really want to have?

What do you think?

Why is Any Many Monster unhappy?
How are Any Many and Many More
monsters different?

The Pumpkin Party

Meg and her dad were playing ball.
Meg calls it soccer,
while her dad calls it football.
Dad kicked the ball at the goal.

"Goal!" he yelled.
"No!" cried Meg, as the ball knocked
down a pot of flowers. CRASH!

Meg and Dad brushed the bits of pot
and soil and flowers up.
"I think we had better stop football
now," said Dad. "Come on,
we'll put some seeds in."

Meg liked helping her dad in the
garden. They grew all sorts of things.
In the shed, they looked at the
packets of seeds.
"This one," said Meg, picking one out.

They put soil into some pots and Meg popped a seed into each one. The seeds were big, flat and white.

Then they wrote the name of the seeds on the markers and put them in the pots too.

When the seedlings had about four leaves each, Meg and her dad put them out into the garden.
"Right then," said Dad, "you had better give them a drink to get them off to a good start."

By the time summer arrived,
everything in the garden was getting
bigger. Meg stood and looked at
her patch of garden.

"They are doing well,"
commented her dad.

"We should write your name on one of the small ones and see what happens when it grows," said Dad. "I used to do that when I was a boy."

So Meg scratched her name onto one of the small pumpkins.

"That really is a fine crop of pumpkins you have grown," said Dad. "What are you going to do with them all?"

"We will never eat *all* of them," said her brother, Josh, as he carried a tray of drinks out. They all sat down and looked at the pumpkins.

"Anyway," continued Josh, "forget pumpkins. The thing I want to know is what sort of birthday party you are going to have. I bet it will be a soccer party. You have a soccer party every time!"

"Well, I'm not going to this time," said
Meg. "This time, I want a... er... a...,"
she looked around, "a different sort
of party," she finished.

"You have a soccer party every time,"
said Josh, and smiled.

On the morning of her party,
Meg and Dad were in the garden,
looking at the pumpkins.

The pumpkin had been small when she
had scratched her name on it,
but now the pumpkin and her name
were much bigger. Her name had
grown with the pumpkin.

Meg picked her pumpkin first, and then
nine more. She collected them up
and took them inside.
"What do you want all of those for?"
said Josh, looking puzzled.
"Wait and see!" replied Meg
with a smile.

At four o'clock, Meg's friends started to arrive. Anna and Kim were first, then Bill, Hinda and Seth.

They went outside to play until the others arrived. Meg unwrapped her presents and thanked everyone for their gifts.

"Right, come inside," said Meg.
"Welcome to my pumpkin party!"
There was a pumpkin for each of them.
"We are going to make our own pumpkin
jack-o'-lanterns," explained Meg.

"The knives are quite sharp," said
Meg's dad, "so go slowly,
and call me if you need help."

When they had finished, they looked at their lanterns. Seth's had lots of pointed teeth, Hinda's had a big smile, and Gus had carved all the way around his.

"They are splendid!" said Meg's dad, as he put a night-light in each one.

They put the jack-o'-lanterns around the room and then they had their party food. Meg had helped to make a pumpkin pie, which everyone tried. Then it was time for the birthday cake.

"I know what shape it will be," said Josh. "It's just got to be a p-"

"A football pitch!" cried everyone,
as the cake was carried in.

"Well!" said Josh, and smiled.
"I said you would get soccer into your
party someway or another!"

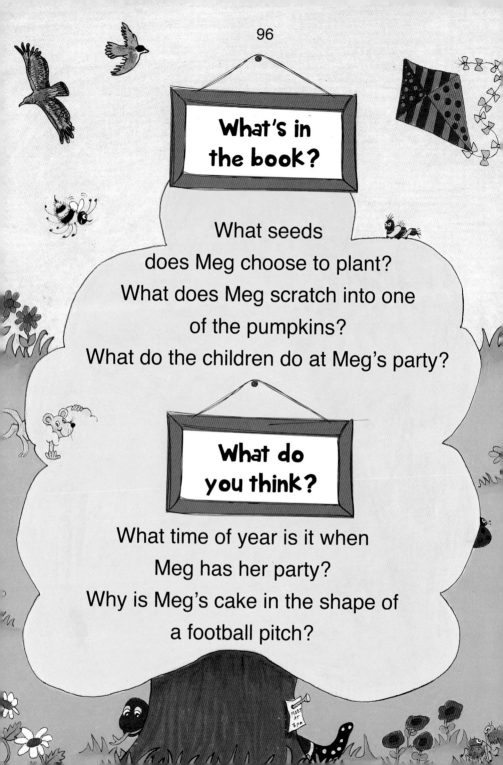

What's in the book?

What seeds
does Meg choose to plant?
What does Meg scratch into one
of the pumpkins?
What do the children do at Meg's party?

What do you think?

What time of year is it when
Meg has her party?
Why is Meg's cake in the shape of
a football pitch?

Town Mouse and Country Mouse

ou

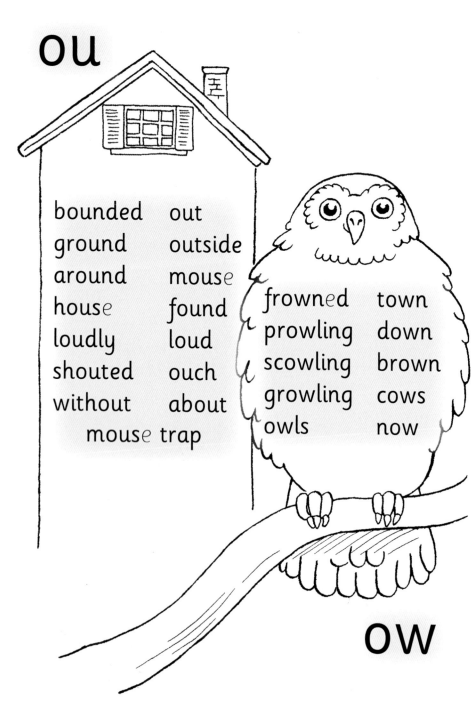

bounded   out
ground   outside
around   mouse
house   found
loudly   loud
shouted   ouch
without   about
mouse trap

frowned   town
prowling   down
scowling   brown
growling   cows
owls   now

ow

The Town Mouse was going to visit
his cousin, who lived in the country.
That morning, he had found a truck
at the market that was going to
where his cousin lived.
Now he was rattling along the lanes,
hidden in the back of the truck.

When he arrived, the Town Mouse
was tired and sore. He clambered out
of the truck and onto the ground.

"There you are! I've been waiting for
you," cried his cousin, the Country
Mouse. "Come on! Come on! Let's get
you home," he continued.

The Country Mouse lived in a hole in a
bank, hidden by a thorny bramble.
"Here we are," said the Country
Mouse, and dived quickly into his hole.

The Town Mouse
started to follow him in.
"Ouch!" he cried,
as he brushed against a thorn.

The Town Mouse was scowling
as he came in.
"You must be very hungry," said the
Country Mouse. "Help yourself.
There is plenty of food."

There were seeds, rose hips, nuts, a big
dish of blackberries and milk to drink.

One evening, when the Town Mouse had been there for about a week, the two sat down for supper.

"Are these the only things you eat?" said the Town Mouse. "Every day, it is the same old food. In the town, we have something different every day," he boasted.

"I would not want to live in the country," he continued. "The cows moo loudly all day. Then the owls hoot as soon as it is dark! It gets so dark by six o'clock that you cannot go outside. Why are there no streetlights?"

The Country Mouse frowned.
"I'm sorry..." he started to say.

"No, I'm sorry," said the Town Mouse.
"It is just that things are so different
where I live. Come to the town with me
and you will see. No cows, no owls and
no scrabbling around looking for food. I
have an enormous house to live in too!"

So the next morning, the Town Mouse
and the Country Mouse found a truck
that was going to the town.
They squeezed in between the crates in
the back of the truck and they munched
on apples all the way there,
while the Town Mouse told his
cousin about life in a town.

It was about two o'clock when they
made their way to the big house,
where the Town Mouse lived.
"Isn't it splendid?" cried the Town
Mouse, pointing to it. The Country
Mouse looked up at the
tall house and nodded.

They were just exploring one of
the bedrooms when there was a
loud growling noise.
"Run!" shouted the Town Mouse.
A big brown dog bounded into the
room and started to chase them. They
reached the mouse hole just in time.

"Let's go to the kitchen and get some
food," said the Town Mouse.
When they got there, the Town Mouse
checked that all was safe.

"No!" he shouted, and ran quickly to the
Country Mouse, who was just about to
grab a big bit of cheese. He knocked the
Country Mouse out of the way, just as
the mouse trap crashed down!

The Town Mouse and the
Country Mouse sat down to eat.
The Country Mouse was still trembling.
There was bread, butter, cheeses
and lots more to eat.

"Now, this is a real feast!" said the
Town Mouse with a smile.
"What would you like to eat?"

The Country Mouse was about to nod and agree with his cousin when he saw something prowling around the corner. "A cat! A cat!" he cried. "Look out!" They scrambled down and made a dash for the mouse hole.

They got there just before the cat.
The Country Mouse was
panting and shivering.

"That's it!" he exclaimed.
"I'm going back to the country.
At least you get your dinner there,
whatever it is, without having to
escape dogs, mouse traps and cats!"

The next morning, the Country Mouse
set off for the country. That evening,
he found himself back in his little hole
in the bank, hidden by brambles.
He sat down, smiled and made himself
an enormous dinner. Then he settled
down to sleep in his safe little bed.

What's in the book?

What does the Country Mouse eat in the country?
How do the mice get to the town?
Where does the Country Mouse find the piece of cheese?

What do you think?

Why doesn't the Town Mouse like the country?
Why doesn't the Country Mouse like the town?

Parents

An important part of becoming a confident, fluent reader is a child's ability to understand what they are reading. Below are some suggestions on how to develop a child's reading comprehension.

Make reading this book a shared experience between you and the child. Try to avoid leaving it until the whole book is read before talking about it. Occasionally stop at various intervals throughout the book.

Ask questions about the characters, the setting, the action and the meaning.

Encourage the child to think about what might happen next. It does not matter if the answer is right or wrong, so long as the suggestion makes sense and demonstrates understanding.

Ask the child to describe what is happening in the illustrations.

Relate what is happening in the book to any real-life experiences the child may have.

Pick out any vocabulary that may be new to the child and ask what they think it means. If they don't know, explain it and relate it to what is happening in the book.

Encourage the child to summarise, in their own words, what they have read.

Book Review

Try to answer these questions about each story in this book:

What was the story about?

What happened at the end of the story? Did you guess what was going to happen?

What was your favourite part of the story? Why did you like it?

Which character did you like the best? Can you describe them?

Did you like the illustrations? Why?

Did any parts of the story make you laugh?

Do you think anyone you know would enjoy this book?

Could you re-tell the story in your own words?

Has anything similar to this story ever happened to you?

Would you have liked this story to be shorter or longer?

Were there any parts of the story that you didn't like?

Have you read any stories that are similar to this one?

Would you enjoy reading this story again and would you recommend it to a friend?

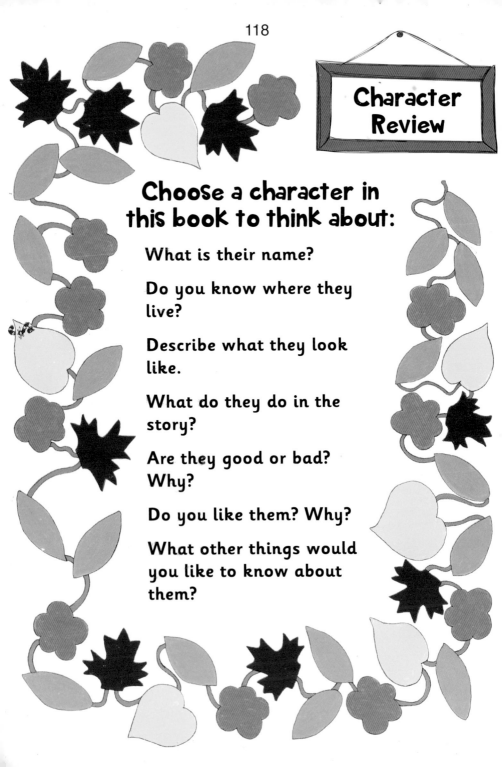

Character Review

Choose a character in this book to think about:

What is their name?

Do you know where they live?

Describe what they look like.

What do they do in the story?

Are they good or bad? Why?

Do you like them? Why?

What other things would you like to know about them?